BRIDAL JEWELLERY

Clare Yarwood-White

A & C Black • London

TITLE PAGE: *Pink crystal necklace by Yarwood-White*

First published in Great Britain in 2007
A & C Black Publishers Limited
38 Soho Square
London W1D 3HB
www.acblack.com

ISBN-10: 07136-7599-3
ISBN-13: 978-0-7136-7599-3

CIP Catalogue records for this book are available from the British Library and the US Library of Congress.

Typeset in 11 on 11.5pt Photina
Book design by Susan McIntyre
Cover design by Sutchinda Rangsi Thompson
Commissioning Editor: Susan Kelly
Copyeditor: Rebecca Faulkner
Proofreader: Julian Beecroft
Index: Sophie Page

Printed and bound in China

This book is produced using paper that is made from wood grown in managed, sustainable forests. It is natural, renewable and recyclable. The logging and manufacturing processes conform to the environmental regulations of the country of origin.

Contents

ACKNOWLEDGEMENTS

Thank you to the following companies for providing photographs of their work: Savoir Design, The Whole Caboodle, Inwater London and Loves Me Loves Me Knot.

Thank you to the following companies for their wine-glass charms: Breast cancer awareness charm and Wedded Bliss charm, Wendy's Wine Charms; bow-shaped charm, Halo's; crystal heart on gold wire, Helpthebride.com; star bead with pearls, Turquoise; pearls with shell heart, Cammar Designs.

The wedding cakes and jewellery by Tracey Mann and Juliana Dutton were first published in *Wedding Cakes – A Design Source*, Squires Kitchen Magazine Publishing.

Special thanks to designer Susan Astaire for contributing her knowledge and photographs. Also to Christine Cowdell, for her valuable creative input, support and constant enthusiasm, and not least for the beautiful photographs.

Finally, the following people have all made contributions for which I am very grateful: Sam Walls, Kate Bamber, Kate Barbour, Rosie Wise, Yvonne Kulagowski, Kate Smallwood, Philippa Richards, Susan Kelly, Erica Higgins and David White.

Introduction

If you think about the most precious possession you own, it may well be jewellery. If you think about the most cherished item of jewellery you own, the chances are it will have links to either your own, or a family, wedding. Bridal jewellery is steeped in meaning and linked to one of the most emotionally charged chapters in a woman's life.

We are all sentimental about jewellery that marks a marriage, whether we treasure the simple string of pearls that belonged to our grandmother, or we are cooing over the diamond ring on the finger of a recently engaged friend.

These pieces often become family heirlooms, regardless of the original cost. The real value lies in the memories they evoke, and the emotional bonds that they represent.

When you design and make jewellery for a bride to wear on her wedding day, you are creating a little piece of history. All eyes will be on the bride, and all camera lenses will be pointed her way. Her beauty will be recorded forever and the little details will make all the difference.

I always feel that working with a bride-to-be at this important time is a real privilege, and an experience which can be exciting and rewarding for both designer and bride. This book has been written to give you an insight into this unique world of wedding jewellery.

If you are new to jewellery design, all the basics are covered to get you started. You will learn about the tools and materials you will need, as well as beading and wire-work techniques that, once mastered, can be used over and over again to create an endless range of designs. There are plenty of simple step-by-step projects which will have you creating beautiful pieces in no time, and you will soon find that by experimenting you can adapt these projects to create truly individual designs. All of the projects in this book can be completed with a few basic hand tools that can be bought through websites or at craft shops, so you will not need lots of specialist equipment to get started.

Perhaps you are the bride-to-be and you want to add a really personal touch to your wedding outfit by making your own jewellery for the big day. Why not go one step further by making co-ordinated gifts for your bridesmaids, or other wedding accessories like cake garlands or wine-glass charms. These are covered in Chapter 6.

If you already have some jewellery-making skills, but would like to learn more about wedding jewellery, Chapter 1 will guide you through the process of consulting and designing, covering everything you need to consider to create the perfect piece of jewellery. Should you decide you want to turn these skills into a career, Chapter 7 and the comprehensive appendix will become a long-term reference source and valuable companion.

1.

Working with Brides

THE SERVICE YOU OFFER

There are a number of different ways to offer your services as a bridal-jewellery designer, and a market for all of them. You may offer one, or a combination, of these as part of your service. Trial and error will establish which way works best for you.

Offering a fixed range of products

You may design and make a fixed range of products, possibly once or twice a year. This may include suites of jewellery built around a particular theme, for example, a silver and crystal tiara with matching earrings, necklace, bracelet and bridesmaids' accessories. You could keep multiples of each item in stock for quick despatch. This service will keep your production economical and simple, allowing you to purchase materials in bulk, and will also avoid costly consultation and design processes. However, you may find there is a limit to how much you can charge for an 'off-the-shelf' range, and you may find it hard to compete with the lowest-cost, factory-manufactured jewellery ranges on the market.

Offering a made-to-order service

You may offer a range of products as above, but would make them to order, allowing customisation of the designs. For example, you could change the colour of the beads in a piece, or alter the length of a necklace or the height of a tiara. You could also allow customers to combine design elements from different ranges. The benefits to you are that you are not left with unsold stock gathering dust, and that you can charge a higher price to cover your design service.

You could offer one design in a range of colours

Offering a bespoke service

This is the 'gold' service, where you design from scratch to suit your client's requirements. It is a time-consuming, and therefore costly, option. You will also most likely require studio space that is suitable for consultations. However, it can be extremely rewarding for the designer, and gives the client the luxury of a truly one-off piece. The rest of this chapter gives you much of the information you need to offer this service.

CONSULTING WITH BRIDES

Wedding and engagement rings and other bridal jewellery

When it comes to designing rings, the bride's entire lifestyle must be taken into account, as these pieces will stay with her forever and need to suit every occasion. For example, a bride who enjoys regular sport may decide to go for a low-profile engagement ring with a bezel setting for practicality. We will talk more about choosing rings in the next chapter.

Bridal jewellery, on the other hand, should be designed to fulfil the dreams of the bride on one significant occasion. This is the type of jewellery discussed below.

The consultation process

When working with brides it is extremely important to be professional, organised and reassuring. This is likely to be one of the biggest emotional journeys a woman has ever embarked on, and consequently she may be feeling somewhat overwhelmed. Your communication and empathy skills are as important here as your design skills, as there is little margin for error on someone's wedding day.

A bride will have many other things on her mind, and choosing her jewellery will be just one of the decisions she will have to make.

Bridal Commission Form

Name

Address

Telephone

Email

Date of wedding

Looking for	For the bride	For the bridesmaids
Tiara	☐	☐
Hairpins	☐	☐
Rings	☐	☐
Earrings	☐	☐
Necklace	☐	☐
Bracelet	☐	☐

Dress: colour, fabric, shape of neckline and skirt

Hair: type, colour, style, hairdresser

Veil: yes or no

Other special or sentimental jewellery, e.g. grandmother's pearls, diamond earrings

Bridesmaids: number, age, colour/style of their dresses

Overall theme/style of wedding, e.g. relaxed, traditional, elegant, funky

Budget

Example enquiry form

However, it is certainly one of the more pleasurable decisions if the designer takes a few simple precautions.

Some clients will come to you with a clear idea of what they want; others will be far less specific, and even confused by the options available to them. Either way, it is important to give your clients confidence in your abilities. These skills will develop with practice, and you will learn how to guide different clients through your own experiences.

Here are some practical pointers to follow when meeting a bride to discuss her jewellery:

- Create a comfortable, organised environment in which to consult with your clients, if possible away from your work bench. They do not need to see 'behind the scenes', as this just takes away some of the magic.
- Listen to your client carefully and give her time to talk to you about her wedding. You will learn a lot about her from this. Ask her what she has already decided on, and what she is looking for in terms of jewellery.
- Make notes: it is easy to forget who said what when you are dealing with a number of clients simultaneously. Design a special 'enquiry form' where you can note down all the relevant information.

- Show the bride samples of your work, and if possible get her to try them on. Often brides change their mind about an item once they are wearing it.
- Ask what she doesn't like as well as what she does like about a design; sometimes this is easier to do and it can help you refine your ideas.
- Agree timescales. Let her know when you can get back to her with design ideas and costs, and make sure she is aware of your deadline for ordering.
- Follow up with a written proposal or design brief outlining designs, materials, costs and any other relevant information.

Design considerations

Make sure you ask the relevant questions of your bride about her style and the plans for the wedding, so that you can take these elements into consideration when creating your designs.

The bride's style

Presumably if a bride has made an appointment to see you it is because she has seen and liked examples of your work. However, every bride is unique and will have different requirements.

Avoid the temptation to talk the bride into a full set of jewellery if this isn't right for her. It is a big responsibility to help dress a woman for her wedding day, and it is your job as a professional to help her get it right. Less is usually more, and besides, one elaborate feature piece of jewellery with subtle complementary pieces often has more impact. People will ask about her jewellery on the day, and you want them to be saying good things about you.

Jewellery should balance with the dress and the style of the bride. The bride will have chosen her dress in keeping with how she wants to feel on the day; elegant, classic, traditional, glamorous or relaxed. It is useful to go through a list of these words with your client to establish how she would like to look and feel. You can then use these to contribute to your design brief.

The dress

In most cases the bride will not be in a position to commit to her bridal jewellery until she has chosen her wedding dress. To avoid wasting your valuable time, it is a good idea to check that she has made this decision, and ask her to bring a picture of the dress to the consultation. Otherwise you may find that she is 'browsing' rather than making any firm decisions. Brides by nature usually like to shop around, and the nearer you can get to decision-making time, the more likely you are to gain a confirmed order.

There are a number of design features on a dress that you should take into account when designing bridal jewellery:

- The neckline: It is good to echo the shape of the neckline in a necklace. A v-neck suits a pendant or drop-style necklace. A round neck looks better with a round necklace or choker. A strapless or square neckline works with most shapes of necklace.
- Beadwork, embroidery or other detail: If the dress features crystals or pearls, you may want to suggest including something similar in the jewellery design. If the bodice features scroll patterns or floral motifs, these can be echoed in the jewellery. Likewise, a heavily scrolled tiara may look at odds with a straight column dress with very clean lines, which could work better with a simple, modern design.

Veil and hair

Consider the beadwork on the dress when designing jewellery

Check whether the bride is wearing a veil, and what she would like to wear in her hair. It is also important to know where the veil will be secured. If it is on top of the head, it will usually look better with a tiara in front of it to conceal the comb. If it will be fastened lower on the head (for example, under a low bun) there is more scope for hair ornaments elsewhere.

Ask your bride if she is planning to have a hairdresser on the day, then you can liaise with him or her about hair accessories in advance. There is no point in designing a heavy tiara, to discover the bride plans to wear her hair loose and the hairdresser has no way to anchor the head-dress.

Tip: Remember to match the colour of any pins or grips you use to your bride's hair colour.

As a general rule, for loose hairstyles, headbands, hair grips and very light tiaras work best. With a very structured up-style, anything goes! Again, the hairdresser may have a preference for ornaments on grips or pins.

Find out if the bride will have a hairdresser on the day

Other jewellery

Another important question to ask is whether the bride is planning on wearing any other special or sentimental jewellery, for example, her mother's pearl necklace or a sentimental pair of diamond ear studs. You will need to take this into consideration when creating your design. She may well be wearing jewellery as her 'something old/new/borrowed/blue'.

The wedding

You should by now have a good feel for the type of bride you are dealing with, but it is worth finding out a bit more about her wedding to help you with your design. Where is the wedding taking place, and at what time of year? Is the bride planning a large, formal affair or a relaxed wedding on a Caribbean beach?

It is always helpful to know if there is a colour scheme for the wedding, as this will also tell you something about the bride's personality. If the chosen colour scheme is dark red, the bride may need bold, dramatic accessories to balance the look.

Bridesmaids

Ask about bridesmaids. Jewellery is a traditional gift from the wedding couple to the bridesmaids, and they may want something they can wear on the day. This way you can carry the theme of the wedding jewellery through to the bridesmaids, creating a co-ordinated look.

Think about the overall style of the wedding

You may want to incorporate colours from the wedding flowers

The same applies to the mother of the bride and the groom's mother. Usually they are given a thank-you gift at the reception. This is often flowers, but a co-ordinating brooch or pair of earrings is a longer-lasting memento of the special day.

A word of warning, though: even if the bridesmaids' jewellery is similar in style to the bride's, find a way to tone it down, or make a smaller version. The bride should always have the most beautiful and stunning dress and flowers, and the same goes for her accessories.

Try different designs

Finally, the best way for you both to see what suits the bride is by her trying on some of your samples. Remind a bride that although a tiara may feel over the top when tried on with her jeans, when she is wearing her wedding gown it will look much more at home.

You should learn to judge what height and profile of tiara suits which face shape; that chokers only really look good on very long, slim necks; that long earrings generally are more elegant without a necklace. Do bear in mind, however, that rules are made to be broken, so look hard at the overall picture and trust your instincts.

THE DESIGN BRIEF

Following the consultation with your bride, you will probably need to take some further time to gather all your information and ideas, draw on your own creativity and come up with the perfect designs for your client.

You will then need to provide a proposal or design brief to confirm the details to your client. You will develop your own style depending on the type of work you undertake, but here are some of the key points it should include:

- Your name and contact details
- The name and contact details of the client
- A description of the jewellery
- Visuals (sketches or photographs of similar work marked with the copyright symbol ©, followed by your name and the current year)
- Materials (descriptions, pictures or samples of beads)
- Measurements (the length of a necklace or height of a tiara)
- A cost breakdown, including details of any design fees, postage and packaging
- Your terms of trade (the amount of deposit required, the date when the balance is due)
- The delivery date

- Your signature and space for the client's signature.

You may find that the design brief needs to be revised as the client makes decisions or changes her mind, but do make sure you have her full agreement and a deposit before starting work. Leave nothing to chance. This will act as a contract between you and your client, and will help protect you in the event of a misunderstanding.

Tip: Contact the client after her wedding to congratulate her, and ask for a photograph of her wearing your jewellery. The picture will be useful for your portfolio, and you will hopefully also receive a thank-you note, which you can use as a testimonial.

FAMILY JEWELLERY

You may be asked to remodel or work with an existing piece of family or sentimental jewellery. For example, a bride may want to wear her grandmother's pearls, but finds that the length of the necklace is out of fashion, or does not suit her neckline. You could simply restring the necklace, and make any extra pearls into a bracelet, or, with the addition of other beads and crystals, completely remodel it into a tiara or hair pins.

A string of ivory pearls has been remodelled by adding bronze pearls and crystal rondells

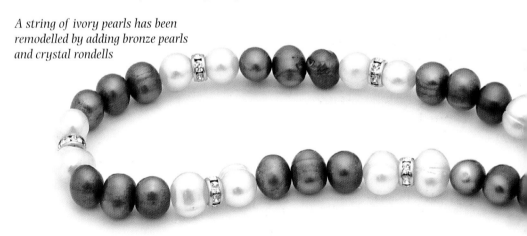

However, do make sure, if you are going to be making irreversible changes to a piece of jewellery, that you clearly explain this in writing beforehand.

This is a wonderful way for the bride to feel the presence of her sentimental jewellery, without compromising on style.

2.

Materials and Tools

If you have never bought jewellery-making tools or materials before, you may wonder where to start. The Internet is a great place, and a simple search for 'beads' will return many jewellery-making websites where you can compare prices and shop online. Some mail-order companies produce catalogues or brochures; they may make a charge for these, but it is useful to keep them for reference.

MATERIALS

It is also worth using the Internet to search for craft and bead shops or gem shows and exhibitions in your area. Although mail-order shopping is convenient, touching, feeling and comparing the materials in person is a great way to spark your design ideas.

Scour markets, antique shops and charity shops for second-hand jewellery. You may be able to recycle a fabulous clasp or feature bead from something that looks fairly ordinary at first glance. This is especially fun for creating one-of-a-kind designs with a vintage feel.

If you are already buying materials from a retailer, find out if they offer discounts for wholesale purchases. You will usually have to buy in greater quantities, but it will make it more cost-effective.

Precious metals

A wedding ring is designed to last a lifetime of everyday wear. For both practical and symbolic reasons it needs to be made from appropriately durable materials.

Platinum is the most expensive and durable metal. It will not tarnish or become misshapen. However, it is more difficult to work with than gold due to its hardness and high melting temperature.

Tip: If a wedding band and engagement ring are to be worn together, choose the same metal for both to prevent one eroding the other.

Gold is also a good choice, but is not used in its pure form for jewellery as it would be too soft. 24-carat gold is considered 'pure',

Platinum and yellow-gold ring (BACK); yellow-gold ring (FRONT), from Susan Astaire

while 18-carat gold has 18 parts gold to 6 parts of another metal. Once gold has been alloyed with other metals such as copper or silver to create the required hardness and colour, it will also stand the test of time.

Other metals, such as silver or copper, are likely to wear thin or misshape over time due to their softness, so are not good choices for wedding bands.

Likewise, an engagement ring needs to be durable. Although it may not be worn every day like a wedding band, gold or platinum are still the preferred metals for the reasons given above.

Gemstones

Since the 15th century, diamonds have been the traditional choice for engagement rings. A diamond is rare, precious and enduring; the perfect symbol for true love.

Today, the value of a diamond is measured by the four Cs: cut, carat, colour and clarity. Cut is a manufactured quality; the others are all naturally inherent in the stone. You can read more about the 4 Cs in Chapter 3.

A distinction is commonly made between precious and semiprecious gemstones. Diamonds, rubies, emeralds and sapphires are referred to as 'precious' because of their relative rarity, with 'semiprecious' being used to describe all other gems. However, there is some debate within the jewellery industry regarding this term, as a large and near-perfect tourmaline stone can be of greater value than a low-grade ruby, for example.

Diamonds, rubies, emeralds and sapphires, otherwise known as precious gemstones

Gemstones are generally valued according to a combination of weight, size, colour, perfection and brilliance. Coloured stones are popular combined with diamonds in engagement rings.

Organic gemstones

Organic gems are distinguished from gemstones as they are formed by once-living organisms. Coral, amber and jet all fall into this category, but the most celebrated in bridal jewellery must be the pearl.

Pearls are formed when an irritant such as a grain of sand enters the shell of a living mollusc. In order to protect itself, the animal adds layer upon layer of nacre to the foreign particle, which eventually builds up to create a pearl. Pearls can naturally occur in a range of colours including white, pink or peach, grey, black and creamy-yellow.

Naturally occurring pearls are extremely rare and expensive, but cultured pearls, where the irritant is deliberately introduced to the mollusc, are widely available in all shapes and sizes. As well as round, potato, pear or rice-shaped pearls you may also come across sticks, coins, crosses or squares.

Tip: Many freshwater pearls are dyed to give them unusual colours such as peacock-green, gold or pink. If you are unsure whether your pearls are naturally coloured or dyed, check the string that the pearls are sold on. If the pearls have been dyed the string will probably show traces of dye.

Ivory freshwater pearls

The pearl is the only gem that does not need to be cut or polished to improve its appearance. Pearls, like Venus the goddess of love, are born of the sea and are symbolic of everlasting love. Coupled with their universally flattering iridescence and soft white colour, they are the perfect choice for brides.

Crystals

The crystal used in jewellery is made from glass, with the addition of lead oxide. The lead adds weight and brilliance, and makes it more suitable for cutting. When beads are cut from crystal the facets give a wonderful sparkle as they catch the light, in the same way that a cut diamond or other gemstone sparkles.

Crystal beads are often embroidered onto wedding gowns or scattered on veils, so incorporating them into jewellery can really complete the bridal look.

Swarovski crystals

Swarovski is possibly the most well- known manufacturer of crystal, and their beads are widely used in fashion and accessories by some of the top designers. They produce a huge range of coloured crystals in a variety of shapes and sizes.

Other materials

Although pearls, gemstones and crystals seem to be the most popular choice for bridal jewellery, there are many other exciting materials that can be used in your designs, especially when designing for bridesmaids or less traditional brides.

Chiffon, velvet, lace or satin ribbon make beautiful chokers and necklaces. Haberdashery stores also stock feathers, flowers and trims that make great head-dresses. Ribbon can also be used for wrapping around tiara bands to create a neat finish.

Mother-of-pearl (the iridescent inside layer of a shell) can be carved into pretty shapes such as flowers and leaves. Beads of glass, metal and wood are plentiful, and second-hand shops can be great places to pick up vintage beads, brooches and trinkets that can be remodelled and updated.

Wire, thread and chains

Silver-plated or gold-plated wire is available in a number of different thicknesses, and will be a staple ingredient of your tiaras and more sculptural jewellery designs. 0.4 mm diameter (26 gauge) wire is flexible

A necklace made with ribbons, gemstones, glass, pearls and crystals, by Yarwood-White

CLOCKWISE, FROM BOTTOM RIGHT:
Ring-size memory-wire coil;
1 mm (18 gauge) silver-plated wire; 0.4 mm
(26 gauge) gold-filled wire; nylon-coated
wire, gold colour; nylon-coated wire,
steel colour; polyester thread, gold
colour; polyester thread, ivory colour;
0.16 mm (34 gauge) wire, silver
colour; 0.16 mm (34 gauge) wire,
gold colour

Tip: Always use memory-wire cutters to cut memory wire, which is a very hard wire, and will blunt your normal wire cutters.

and great for threading beads, twisting and creating links. 1 mm diameter (18 gauge) wire is a bit sturdier, and useful for creating tiara bands.

Silk and polyester threads, steel wire, nylon and elastic are all useful threading materials for making necklaces or bracelets. Your choice of thread will depend on the size and weight of the beads you are using, the size of their holes, and the way your design is intended to hang.

Memory wire always springs back to its original shape, and can be bought in necklace, bracelet or ring sizes. It is good for making bangles or chokers, and the smaller ring-sized coil can be used for making wine-glass charms. Special capping beads are available for finishing the ends.

Findings

Findings are the other components you will use in your jewellery, and include clasps, jump rings, earring hooks or posts, chains and pins. Some jewellers will make these items by hand, using their metalwork skills. Although this is time-consuming, it is a wonderful way to add a unique, hand-finished style to a design. This will of course be reflected in the price of the finished piece.

As an alternative, a wide range of these components are available on the market for designers who want to complete their designs in a shorter time frame. These findings are often gold-plated or silver-plated, gold-filled (a base metal with a layer of gold bonded to it, also known as rolled gold), vermeil (sterling silver with a gold plate), sterling silver or 9-carat gold. Some common findings are described below:

- *Lobster/trigger clasp*: A secure clasp, used for necklaces and bracelets.
- *Ball clasp*: Pretty on strings of pearls, but harder to do up on a bracelet without help.
- *Toggle clasp*: Used for heavy necklaces, but less secure on bracelets.
- *Closed jump ring*: Soldered into a complete ring, used with a lobster clasp to close a necklace or bracelet.
- *Open jump ring*: Can be prised open with pliers, used to add clasps to a chain, or secure charms to a chain.
- *Ear post and butterfly*: Secure, neat earring finding, good for classic designs.
- *Ear wire or hook*: A more contemporary earring finding, works well with long chandelier-style or heavier earrings.
- *Head pin or ball pin*: A wire with a head or ball at one end, beads are added to create charms.
- *Headband*: Useful for making Alice-style headbands, but not ideal for tiaras (see Chapter 4 for more information).
- *Gimp*: A tiny coil of wire used to protect the thread when stringing beads, also known as French wire.
- *Spacer bar*: Used for separating rows in multi-strand designs such as chokers.
- *Crimps*: Tiny metal tubes that can be threaded onto steel wire or nylon and flattened with pliers to secure beads or clasps.

BEAD AND WIRE-WORK TOOLS

All of the jewellery shown and the projects demonstrated in this book, with the exception of wedding and engagement rings, can be made with a few simple hand tools. Some of these are described below:

- *Round/ring-nose pliers*: These have circular jaws and are used for bending wire and headpins to make loops.
- *Flat/chain-nose pliers*: Used for opening and closing jump rings, squeezing crimps and flattening wire wraps. Nylon-coated jaws are good for protecting softer wire from marks.
- *Wire cutters*: A good pair of wire cutters will trim wire neatly, and avoid sharp, scratchy ends.
- *Scissors*: For trimming threads, ribbons, feathers and so on.
- *Glue*: Two-part epoxy glue and superglue for fixing stones, crystals, etc. to fittings, and gluing ribbons or textiles. Check with the manufacturer's recommendations for the correct glue for the job.
- *Beading needles*: Made of fine, flexible wire for stringing pearls and beads. The eye collapses when pulled through a bead.
- *Matches or lighter*: For sealing the ends of polyester knots when threading beads.
- *Tape measure*: For sizing your jewellery.

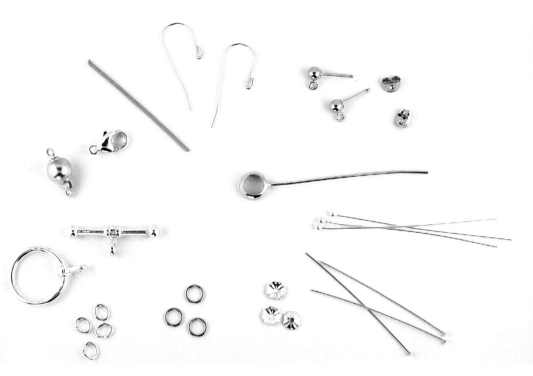

CLOCKWISE FROM TOP: *Sterling-silver ear hooks; gold-filled earring posts and butterfly backs; sterling-silver pendant bail; sterling-silver ball pins; gold-filled head pins; sterling-silver bead caps; gold-filled soldered jump rings; sterling-silver open jump-rings; sterling-silver toggle clasp; sterling-silver ball clasp; sterling-silver lobster clasp; gold gimp or French wire*

CLOCKWISE FROM BOTTOM: *Memory-wire cutters; wire cutters; round-nose pliers; flat-nose pliers*

CLOCKWISE FROM BOTTOM: *Beading needles, tape measure, lighter, scissors*

3.

Engagement and Wedding Rings

Engagement and wedding rings differ from the jewellery covered in the rest of this book. They are known as fine jewellery, that is, jewellery made using precious metals and stones, and requiring specialist production methods and equipment.

Most of the techniques described for making tiaras and other jewellery can be carried out with a few hand tools and some practice, whereas making rings requires equipment for cutting, shaping, soldering, stone setting and polishing, as well as a good level of knowledge and skill to work safely.

There are plenty of good books that cover these techniques in more detail, and also a variety of practical short courses where you can learn the skills. There are even workshops where couples can go for a day to make their own wedding rings.

HISTORY AND SYMBOLISM OF RINGS

There are many speculative ideas about the history of engagement and wedding rings, and when and where the first rings were exchanged. Some sources tell of cavemen giving bands of reeds to their women, and less romantic tales of the ring as a sign of the woman's slavery. Later, engagement rings probably represented part of a bride's dowry, and a symbol of a man's honourable intentions.

Archduke Maximillian of Hamburg gave a diamond engagement ring to Mary of Burgundy in 1477, and this is often cited as the time when this tradition became popular.

Today, the rings share a common meaning across many cultures. The circle is unbroken, with no beginning or end, symbolising an enduring love and commitment, and the wedding ring is worn constantly as a reminder of the vows a couple have taken.

Diamonds are the hardest and most long-lasting stone, making them the most popular choice for engagement rings, for both symbolic and practical reasons.

Although historically the wedding ring was presented by a man to a woman, it is now common for a couple to exchange wedding rings, which are worn on the third finger of the left hand. The ancient Egyptians believed that the vein in this finger connected directly to the heart. When a woman wears an engagement and wedding ring together, she puts the wedding band on first, so that it sits closest to the heart.

DESIGN CONSIDERATIONS: ENGAGEMENT RINGS

Choosing an engagement ring can be particularly tricky for a man, torn between wanting to keep the element of surprise and not wanting to make a costly mistake. There are some simple pointers a designer can use to help him make the right choice:

- Does his prospective bride normally prefer to wear silver/white-gold jewellery or yellow-gold? Many women have a strong preference for one or the other, and it is easy to check by looking at her favourite pieces.
- What style of jewellery does she favour: traditional or contemporary,

A contemporary sapphire engagement ring

elaborate or simple? Does she suit chunky rings or finer, more delicate bands?

- Would she want a classic diamond, or perhaps a more unusual coloured-stone design?
- Does she wear her jewellery all the time, including when sleeping or playing sport?
- Has she admired a friend's ring, or one in a shop window? Often a woman will have dropped some heavy hints about the ring of her dreams; it is just a case of listening out for them.
- In addition, consider her personality, her dress style, her hobbies and lifestyle.

Similar questions can be asked of a woman if she is choosing the ring herself, to help her narrow down the choice.

DESIGN CONSIDERATIONS: WEDDING RINGS

In addition to some of the questions above, when choosing wedding rings, a couple should consider the following:

- Do they want their rings to match, or would they be happy to have different-coloured metals or designs? This is really a matter of personal preference.
- Do they want diamonds or stones in their wedding bands? Will they want to have them engraved? Designs set with stones can sometimes be harder to engrave.

- Will the bride want to wear her engagement ring with her wedding band, or will she transfer it to the other hand? They should look balanced together, and sit comfortably side by side, without one overpowering the other.
- Will the groom want to match his ring to the colour of his watch?

Tip: Make sure your ring is sized correctly before you have it engraved, as resizing could disorder the message.

Susan Astaire is a leading London jewellery designer who has specialised in custom-made engagement and wedding rings for over twenty years. During that time she has worked with rock stars, film stars and royalty. She suggests offering the following advice to couples choosing their wedding bands:

- Make sure the ring is not too contemporary in style. High fashion dates, and this is a long term purchase that you still want to love in twenty years' time. My favourite style is modern-classic; it looks equally great now and in the future.
- Buy the finest-quality ring that you can afford, as quality will always stand the test of time.
- Go for platinum if the budget will allow. Its looks will last a lifetime and it will not change colour or tarnish. 18-carat white gold has a lower initial outlay and looks beautiful when the ring is new, but needs maintenance in the form of re-polishing and plating every couple of years.
- Diamond-set wedding bands will look much prettier than plain ones after the initial shine has worn off the ring. You will still be left with a lovely sparkle from the stones, whereas an all-metal ring may look dull and scratched after a few years.
- Try the wedding ring on its own without the engagement ring next to it. You may have occasions when you just want to wear a single band (particularly if you have a high, claw-set engagement ring), for example, when gardening or during babycare. Make sure you like the ring by itself as well as in a pair.
- Go by your gut instinct. If you love a ring straight away you will probably like it above all the others that you see while trekking around. Don't worry about buying the first ring you see if you feel it is the right one.

18-carat white and yellow gold and diamond three-row ring, and platinum and diamond one-row ring by Susan Astaire

CHOOSING THE METAL

Gold

If the preferred design is gold, the choice would usually be between 14-carat, 18-carat and 24-carat. Gold is combined with other metals before it can be practically used for jewellery-making and the carat refers to the number of parts of gold per thousand.

the most pure is 24-carat, but for that reason it is also the softest, so not really a good choice for a ring that needs to last a lifetime. 18-carat is usually recommended for wedding or engagement rings as it strikes a balance between quality and durability, containing 18 parts gold and 6 parts other metal.

White gold is made by increasing the amount of white alloys (usually silver or palladium) in the gold, and rose gold by adding more copper.

Platinum

Platinum is harder and rarer than gold, and consequently more expensive. It won't tarnish, fade or wear away. It is denser and heavier than gold, and can be more difficult to work with. All of this will be reflected in the higher cost of a platinum ring.

Metal can be polished in different ways to create a highly reflective surface, or a more contemporary satin or matt finish.

In recent years white gold and platinum have become a very popular choice for wedding and engagement rings.

SIZING

Ideally you would take a measurement in person using a ring-sizing device, but this is not always possible, especially if there is an element of surprise involved for an engagement ring. There are a number of other tricks you can recommend to the groom-to-be in order to get an accurate measurement:

- 'Borrow' one of the rings from her jewellery box (sneak a look at which finger she normally wears it on) and take it to a local jeweller to be sized.
- Make a photocopy of one of her rings, making sure the copier is set to actual size. This can then be measured by a jeweller.
- Try the ring on, and see how far down your finger it goes. Make a mark, and then go to a jeweller for a measurement.
- If in doubt about the exact size, it is probably best to go up a size, as it is fairly straightforward to have a ring made smaller if it doesn't fit.

If you can take a ring measurement in person, do bear in mind that fingers may swell slightly in warmer weather. Also, if the final ring will be much wider than the measuring tool, you will need to increase the size for it to move comfortably over the knuckle.

THE FOUR CS

As mentioned in Chapter 2, diamonds are commonly graded by the four Cs. This is helpful when comparing diamonds, and assessing value for money. Some famous jewellers pride themselves on only working with the highest-grade diamonds in terms of colour and clarity. A diamond that rates highly in the four Cs will display brilliance (white light), dispersion (rainbow-coloured light or fire) and scintillation (sparkle when the diamond moves).

Carat

Carat is a unit of weight, so the heavier the diamond, the higher the carat. One carat is equal to 0.2 grams. Each carat is divided into 100 points. The term 'carat' derives from the Greek for carob, as carob seeds were once used as a measuring unit on scales. Diamonds become rarer, and therefore more valuable, the heavier they get.

The largest diamond ever mined was the Cullinan, found in South Africa in 1905 and named after Sir Thomas Cullinan, who owned the mine. It weighed 3106.75 carats before it was cut into the Great Star of Africa, weighing 530.2 carats, the Lesser Star of Africa, which weighs 317.40 carats, and many other smaller diamonds.

Colour

Diamonds naturally occur in a wide variety of colours, including pink, green, blue and yellow. The most desirable diamonds are at either end of the spectrum: white or 'colourless', or the strongest, deepest-coloured stones, known as fancy diamonds. White diamonds are graded from D to Z, according to the quality of their colour. D to F are considered colourless grades, and G to J near colourless. Colourless diamonds reflect light better, and with good clarity and a good cut will be quite dazzling.

Pink and yellow diamond rings

Clarity

Naturally occurring flaws within diamonds can take the form of spots, flecks, clouds or cracks, either within the stone or externally. Diamonds are graded on a scale according to the size and location of these imperfections or inclusions. Flawless diamonds contain no visible inclusions when magnified by ten times, and are graded IF for 'internally flawless'. The lowest grade has flaws that can be seen by the naked eye.

Cut

Rough gemstones are cut and polished after they have been mined to create many little faces or facets. Cutting is a precision skill using mathematical formulae, as poorly cut stones will not refract light properly, and will lose their lustre.

Although the facets reflect light through the stone, the overall depth of the stone is important too. If the diamond is cut too deep or too shallow, it will appear dull or dark, as light will leak through the sides, rather than bouncing back through the top of the stone. Many cuts have been patented by their designers and are used to differentiate diamonds in a generic market.

Obviously cutting also affects the overall shape of the diamond. Popular shapes for engagement rings include round, marquise, emerald, princess, pear and oval. These are often seen as solitaires, although more commonly now engagement rings feature smaller diamonds on the side such as baguette or trillion cut.

SETTING

The setting refers to the arrangement of the stone or stones in the ring, and the method used to hold them in place. The design of the setting can dramatically affect the feel of the same stone. For example, a round solitaire in a claw setting will look classic and traditional, but the same stone in a wide-band gypsy setting is very contemporary.

The design considerations we talked about earlier will help establish the most appropriate setting.

FROM TOP: *Bezel, tension, grain and frame-set diamond rings at Susan Astaire*

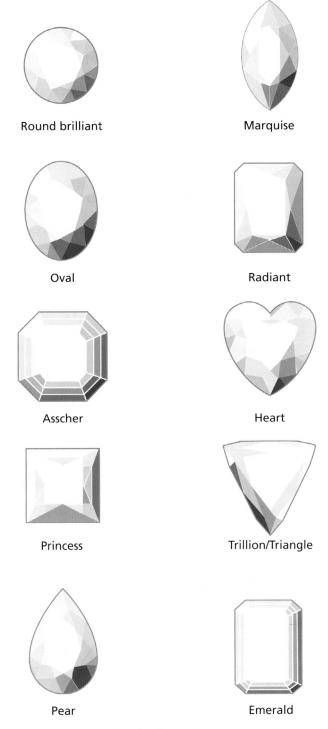

Round brilliant

Marquise

Oval

Radiant

Asscher

Heart

Princess

Trillion/Triangle

Pear

Emerald

Popular diamond cuts

Claw setting

The claw setting is probably the most commonly used setting. The stone is held in place with a number of prongs, usually between two and six. The claws can be small and discreet, to allow the stone to shine through, or else a more ornate design feature of the ring. Either way, the claws should sit flush to the stone to hold it securely and evenly in place, and to avoid the ring snagging on clothing.

Channel setting

Often used for wedding and eternity rings, or on the shoulders of an engagement ring. In this setting the stones are placed next to each other, with no metal in between. They are held in place by parallel walls of metal either side of the row of stones. Channel setting works particularly well with straight-edged stones such as princess or baguette cut.

A claw-set platinum engagement ring with channel-set shoulders, and matching channel-set wedding ring, by Susan Astaire

A bezel-set diamond and platinum engagement ring with gypsy-set diamond shoulders and matching gypsy-set wedding band, by Susan Astaire

Bezel setting

This is also known as a rub-over setting. The stone is surrounded by a wall of metal which is then pushed down over the edge of the stone to hold it in place. Bezel settings can have straight or ornamental edges. Bezel settings are good for protecting softer stones like opals.

Gypsy setting

This is a variation of the bezel setting, where the stone is set flush into the ring. It is popular for setting stones into men's wedding rings, and also a practical choice for an active lifestyle, as it will protect the stone and won't catch on clothing.

Tension setting

The stone is held in place by the pressure of the metal either side of it, and will appear to float when viewed from the side. Although the design can look delicate, if set properly a tension-held stone is very secure.

Tension-set diamond ring

BELOW: *A bar-set baguette diamond and platinum engagement ring with matching wedding band, by Susan Astaire*

Bar setting

This is a version of the channel setting, where short bars are used between the stones, leaving the sides exposed.

Illusion setting

The metal surrounding the stone is faceted to reflect light, thereby making the stone look larger than it is. Alternatively, a number of small stones can be clustered together to give the appearance of one larger one.

Pavé setting

In this setting, small stones are set close together, held by tiny prongs of metal. The overall effect is of a glittering paving of stones.

FOREGROUND: *Four princess-cut diamonds are set together to create the illusion of a solitaire in this ring by Susan Astaire*

A pavé-set diamond and white gold ring, by Susan Astaire

4.

Tiaras and Head-dresses

There is something very special about wearing a tiara or head-dress that makes every woman feel like royalty. It takes us back to our childhood days of dressing-up boxes and princess crowns, and for many women their most romantic and glamorous dreams come true when they walk up the aisle wearing one.

A head-dress endorses a bride's status as queen for the day and sets her apart from her normal life and indeed her other guests. I know a bride who married years ago, but still wears her tiara to give her confidence and poise when making difficult phone calls!

The best way for a bride to choose a tiara is by trying on a range of samples to see what suits her best. Take time to discuss the different styles with your client during the initial consultation, as this will help avoid costly and disappointing mistakes.

HEAD-DRESS STYLES

The common head-dress styles are described below:

Tiara

Worn towards the front of the hair in an upright position, or further back in front of a bun or veil

Headband

Worn Alice-band style, across the top of the head from ear to ear

Hair pin

Suitable for arranging in structured up-styles

Hair grip

Ideal for short or loose hair

Comb

Can be worn tiara-style, or used with feathers and beads for a less formal look

Crown

A style with a historical, even fairytale feel, secured with grips

DECIDING ON A HEAD-DRESS TYPE

When deciding on a style of head-dress, there are a number of important factors to take into consideration.

Hair

The first thing to find out about is the bride's hair type and style. This is crucial to the comfort of the bride on her wedding day, as a poorly thought-through design that is difficult to secure will wobble and make her feel awkward.

Many brides will choose to wear their hair in some kind of up-style, and as a rule this gives you the widest scope for designing a head-dress, as it is much easier to anchor hair accessories into a structured hairstyle, than into loose hair. If the hair will be worn loose, or is very short or fine, it may be better to recommend a headband which will support itself, and keep the weight of the hair accessories as light as possible.

Depending on how far forward the bride will be positioning her tiara, you will need to shorten or lengthen the tiara band accordingly. A heavy tiara may require a longer band to balance it and secure it in place.

Ask the bride whether she wants the detail to be at the back of her head or visible from the front. If the bride is wearing a veil, a tiara or comb, arranged at the front is a good option. If there is no veil, there is more scope to wear accessories on the back of the head. This type of style is great for adding interest to the back view; one that the bride's guests will be looking at throughout the wedding ceremony.

Find out if there will be a hairdresser present on the wedding day. Again, heavier tiaras need skill to position and secure, and I would not recommend this job was left for the bride to do herself. It may be worth having a discussion with the hairdresser in advance to make sure they can work with the accessories you are designing. For example, they may prefer accessories to be on grips rather than pins.

Make a note of the bride's hair colour so you can match pins, grips or headbands; black pins in blonde hair (or vice versa) are not attractive.

Tip: Heavy tiaras are hard to secure in very short or loose hair. Recommend decorative pins, grips or a headband style instead.

Veil

Another important thing to ask early on is whether the bride will be wearing a veil, and if so where on her head it will be secured. It may sound obvious, but a tiara needs to be positioned in front of the veil.

Face shape

If you are consulting personally with your bride, you should recommend a head-dress that you know will complement her face shape:

- With a round face, a gently inverted v-shaped tiara or one with height will flatter.
- Low headbands or tiaras, or accessories worn on the back of the head, suit long faces.
- Oval faces suit most shapes of head-dress.

MAKING A WIRE-WORK TIARA

There are many different designs or techniques that can be used to create a wire-work tiara, as is demonstrated by the wide range on offer. One of the most appealing things about this style of tiara is that each one is truly a one-off, as although designs can be replicated, no two will be identical.

You will need:

- Beads, pearls or crystals
- 1.0 mm diameter (18 gauge) wire (to make the headband) 0.4 mm (26 gauge) diameter wire (to secure the beads)
- Around 1.5 m of 3 mm wide ribbon (gold, silver or to match the hair colour, but preferably grosgrain, velvet or matt finish rather than satin, which can make the tiara slip)

- Wire cutters
- Round-nose pliers
- Superglue

Creating the headband

I am not a fan of the manufactured headbands that are sold as tiara bands, as they are in most cases too big, inflexible and uncomfortable to wear. You can create the most beautiful design in the world, but if it makes the bride uncomfortable you have fallen short as a designer. The beauty of making your own band is that it will be the perfect length to support the design (the further back the bride wears the tiara, the shorter the band needs to be). A badly fitting tiara will have to be tipped backwards to compensate for the band being too large, and will be uncomfortable and unsightly.

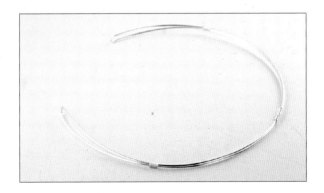

1 Using the 1 mm wire, start with a piece twice as long as your finished headband, for example, 60 cm for a 30 cm band.

Working with the natural curve of the wire, place your round-nose pliers a quarter of the way along the wire, in this case 15 cm. Bend the wire upwards and back on itself around the pliers.

Do the same at the other end of the wire, and you will end up with a 30 cm band, with two neat loops which are vertical to the band.

2 Take a piece of 0.4 mm (26 gauge) wire a few inches long, and use this to bind the two wires securely together at both sides, and across the join in the middle.

Adding the beads

3 Take a piece of 0.4 mm (26 gauge) wire approximately 50 cm long. You will get used to working with a length of wire that suits you, but bear in mind if it is too long it will be unwieldy to manage if it is too short you will have too many joins in your work.

Secure one end to the centre of your tiara band with a few neat wraps.

Make a bend in the wire about 5 cm from the band, and add a bead, pushing it down to the bend. Pinch the bead in one hand, and the wire and band in the other.

4 Gently twist the bead until the two pieces of wire are completely entwined. Be careful not to over-twist, as this can cause the wire to snap. By working with the wire you will quickly get to know how far you can twist before this happens.

5 Wrap the long wire once or twice around the band, and repeat the process above.

Continue adding beads and twisting the wire to create the profile of the tiara. Bear in mind that once the wire has been twisted, it will end up a little shorter than where you originally bent the wire and added the bead, so make the bend slightly higher than you want the finished bead to be.

6 When your first piece of wire runs out, simply secure a new piece with a few wraps, and continue along the band until you have completed both sides.

Tip: To make sure your tiara is symmetrical, start in the centre of your tiara and work outwards to one side, then come back to the middle and match up the other side.

Wrapping the band

Once you are happy with your final design, you can wrap the band in the ribbon to cover your loose ends of wire and give a neat professional finish to the tiara. Wrapping the tiara also helps to anchor your wire twists and make the design more robust.

7 Take your ribbon, and tie it neatly around one of the loops on your band, about 4 cm from the end. Carefully wrap the ribbon around the band, tucking the loose end in, holding it tightly and making sure no wire is exposed.

When you reach the bead work, carefully slide the ribbon between each wire stem. Make sure that the ribbon is pulled tight against the band, and covers all the band work at the front and the back.

8 Continue until you are 4 cm from the other end of the band, tie the ribbon, and secure the knots at each end with a drop of superglue.

Tip: Wait for the superglue to dry before trying on the tiara!

By adding more beads you can create dramatic effects using this technique.

A crystal tiara made using the technique explained above

ADDING TO THE DESIGN

Once you have mastered the technique described above, you will be able to start experimenting with other shapes and designs.

It is possible to create flowers, sprigs, leaves, scrolls and other shapes quite simply with a few extra steps.

Sprigs

1 Bend your 0.4 mm (26 gauge) wire and add a bead as before, but this time pinch the wire halfway down before twisting.

2 Take one of the loose ends, bend again, add another bead, and pinch at the Y point before twisting.

3 You can then go on to add more beads to this sprig, either at the Y point, or lower down, or simply continue twisting to complete the sprig.

Sprigs are great for beginners because they work well in random patterns. Once you master this technique, you can start to have fun with other shapes, such as this fern design.

A pearl tiara made using the sprig technique

Clusters

Another solid effect can be achieved by adding more than one bead to each twist. The technique is very simple. Bend the wire as before, add two or three beads instead of one, then twist as before.

Different effects can be achieved depending on how the wire is bent over the beads, and the number and size of the beads used in each cluster.

Using this technique it is possible to create a design where the wire work is almost invisible behind the beads.

Creating a cluster effect

A tiara created using the cluster technique

Leaves and loops

Leaf, petal and loop shapes can be added by simply threading small beads onto 0.4 mm (26 gauge) wire and looping it over before twisting at the base to secure.

A pearl loop

A headband made with silver pearls and the loop technique

This technique is useful for creating volume within a design, without making it too heavy.

Alternatively, you can create solid beaded leaves and petals with wire using a simple weaving pattern as shown in the diagram below.

These work best with beads around 2–4 mm in size, and with flexible fine wire around 0.16 mm (34 gauge) in diameter.

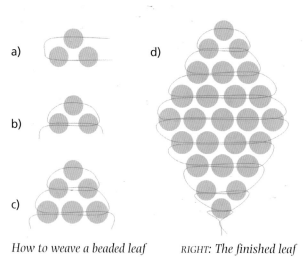

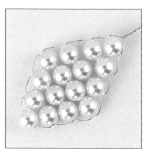

How to weave a beaded leaf   RIGHT: *The finished leaf*

Flowers

Flower effects can be created using pear-shaped beads which have been drilled across the narrow end.

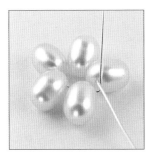 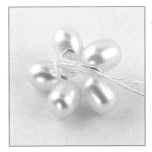 

1 Thread five beads onto a piece of wire and carefully bend it round into a tight loop. Where the wires cross, wrap one behind the other and pull it back up across the centre of the flower.

2 Add a small bead to make the flower centre, and wrap the wire back down the back of the flower.

3 Twist the wires together to create the stem. The flower can then be added to a tiara, headband or hair pin.

A hair grip made using the flower technique

The techniques described above for leaves, loops and flowers can also be added to pins and grips.

Tip: Once a bride has chosen her tiara, suggest matching grips or pins for her bridesmaids.

Making hair pins or grips

The tricky part about making hair pins or grips is attaching the design to the grip. It needs to be done firmly to avoid wobble, but carefully to avoid damaging and snapping the wire. Start by practising with a pin, as these are slightly easier to work with than grips because of their open shape. Once you have mastered pins, you will find it easier to work with grips.

1 To create a pin using the sprig technique, start by wrapping a 50 cm piece of 0.4 mm diameter wire tightly two or three times round the pin. The tighter you can make this, the more stable the design will be, but avoid over-manipulating the wire as this will weaken it. With practice (and probably a few breakages!) you will find the perfect tension.

2 Then simply follow the previous instructions for making sprigs. Once you have added three or four sprigs to each branch, complete the stem by pinching the wires where they meet the pin, and twisting. Then wrap the long wire neatly around the pin once or twice, before starting another branch.

3 Keep going until you have created the desired effect, and finish off with a few more neat but tight wraps. Cut the wire closely. If the sprigs feel a bit wobbly, give the wire wrapped around the pin a very gentle squeeze with flat-nosed pliers, and it should tighten up.

A pin made using the sprig technique

5.

Necklaces, Bracelets and Earrings

The techniques described in this chapter are useful for making necklaces, bracelets and earrings.

WIRE WRAP LOOPS

A wire-wrapped loop is one of the most secure ways to connect beads and findings. Wire loops have many uses, and once you have mastered this technique you will use it again and again in your jewellery designs. The aim is to keep the shape of the loop as round as possible, and vertically in line with the 'neck' of the loop. The wraps should be close together and horizontal to the loop. Practise on scraps of wire to master the technique.

You will need:

- Round-nose pliers
- Flat-nose pliers
- A headpin
- A bead
- Wire cutters

1 Start with the bead on the pin, and place the pliers horizontally and flush to the top of the bead. Bend the wire at a right angle across the top of the pliers.

2 Move the pliers into a vertical position, holding the horizontal wire close to the bend you have just made. Use your free hand to bend the wire over the top of the pliers to form a loop.

3 When the end of the wire gets to a vertical position, swap the loop from the top nose of the pliers to the bottom nose of pliers; this will allow you to finish the bottom of the loop by working the wire round into a horizontal position.

4 Holding the loop flat between your pliers, take the free end of wire with your other hand and wrap it tightly around the neck of the loop two or three times, until you reach the bead. Trim the wire closely. If necessary, squeeze the cut end with flat-nosed pliers for a completely smooth finish.

With practice, you will be able to complete professional-looking and secure loops quickly and easily.

If you are joining pieces together, for example adding charms to a chain to make a charm bracelet, you would thread the chain onto your loop after step 3, and before you start step 4 of this process.

*A charm made with wire
(instructions opposite)*

A selection of beads with wire-wrapped loops

A simple pearl charm bracelet made using chain and wire-wrap charms

You can also make charms using wire instead of headpins (see picture opposite). For example, add three beads to a piece of wire. Pull the ends of the wire towards each other until they cross, then wrap one around the other two or three times and trim the excess. Add a bead to the remaining end, and create a wire-wrap loop by following steps 1 to 4 above.

Making wire-wrap earrings

A simple pearl or crystal drop is always a popular choice of earrings with brides.

You will need:

- A pair of ear posts with loop
- A pair of butterfly earring backs
- Four matching pearl or crystal beads, approximately 6 mm
- Two ball pins
- Two 6 mm crystal rondells
- Round-nose pliers
- Wire cutters
- Flat-nose pliers.

1 Add a pearl, then a crystal rondell, then another pearl to a headpin.

2 Close the loop at the top of the pin using the wrapping technique explained above.

3 Carefully open the loop on the ear post, and add the charm, before gently closing the loop with pliers, being careful not to squash the shape. Repeat for the other earring.

Many different earring designs can be created using the wire-wrapped loop technique, and adding elements such as chain and wire.

In the earrings shown below, 0.4 mm (26 gauge) wire has been used to create a charm with two crystals.

Crystal earrings made with wire

In the earrings shown opposite, above, 0.4 mm (26 gauge) wire has been used to join beads together in a chain formation, and charms have been added to the loops with the wire-wrap loop technique.

The earrings shown opposite, below, are made by attaching a piece of chain to the ear fitting, then adding charms to the chain using jump rings. You could also use the wire-wrap loop technique to add the stones to the chain.

*Drop earrings made
with wire and
headpins*

*Drop earrings with
faceted gemstones*

Making a wire-wrap bracelet

You will need:

- 21 x 6 mm beads
- 26 x 4 mm beads
- Headpins
- 0.4 mm diameter (26 gauge) wire
- Lobster clasp
- Two open jump rings
- One closed jump ring
- Round-nose pliers
- Flat-nose pliers
- Wire cutters

1 Put aside 15 of the 6 mm beads, and 8 of the 4 mm beads. Use the remaining beads to make 16 assorted charms using the headpins and the wire wrap technique described above.

2 Create a loop in the middle of a piece of wire using your round-nose pliers, and secure with two or three twists.

3 Add two of your remaining 6 mm beads to one side of the wire, and one 6 mm bead to the other. Wrap one piece around the other to secure the beads.

4 Trim the excess of the wire you have just wrapped. Then form a loop using the remaining piece of wire, adding two charms to the loop before you close it. You will now have one finished link of your bracelet.

5 Attach a new piece of wire to the link using a wire-wrap loop, positioning it between the two charms.

6 Add two 4 mm beads to the wire, and then form another loop, adding two charms to the loop before you close it.

7 Repeat the process in steps 2 to 6 above, adding new links to your bracelet. Keep going until you have used all the remaining beads, and close the final link with a loop.

8 Using snipe-nose pliers and the open jump rings, add a clasp to the loop at one end of the bracelet, and a closed jump ring to the other, to complete your bracelet.

Tip: When opening jump rings, pull one end towards you and push the other away, rather than pulling them apart in opposite directions, to retain the shape of the ring.

THREADING TECHNIQUES

Knotting pearls

Pearls or other valuable gemstones are often strung with knots between each bead. There are a number of benefits to making jewellery with this technique, the most important being that, should the strand break, usually only one bead will fall off. It can also protect the beads from rubbing against each other, and extend the length of a necklace or bracelet, making expensive beads go further.

The knots will eventually start to fray, stretch or collect dirt, depending on how often the item is worn, so it is worth restringing pearls every couple of years. Brides will often own a sentimental row of family pearls that they would like restrung or remodelled for their wedding, so knotting is a good skill to learn.

Knotting pearls can be tricky at first, but with practice will come naturally. Frustrating mistakes are common, such as cutting the thread too short and only discovering this once you have knotted 90 per cent of the necklace.

Knotting a pearl necklace

You will need:

- Silk or polyester thread
- Wire beading needle
- Clasp (a ball clasp is pretty with round pearls)
- Pearls
- Two pieces of gimp approximately 5 mm long (silver or gold to match your clasp)
- Scissors
- Lighter or matches, or clear nail varnish

Tip: Silk thread will make your pearls drape beautifully. However, it will stretch, fray, absorb grease from the skin and discolour faster than polyester thread.

1 Choose your thread depending on the size of the holes in your pearls. It should be just thick enough that the knots do not slip through the holes, but are as small and discreet as possible.

Knotting between each pearl uses around three times more thread than the same piece would without knots. Also, you will be using the thread double thickness, so you need to cut a piece six times the length of the finished necklace, plus about 40 cm extra to allow for finishing.

Thread your wire needle, level up the two ends of the thread and tie a loose slip knot.

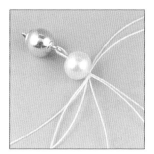

2 Thread one pearl, a piece of gimp and one side of your clasp onto the thread, pulling them up to the slip knot.

Then thread the needle back through the same bead in the opposite direction, forming a loop of gimp around the clasp.

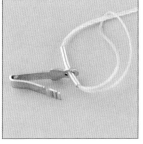

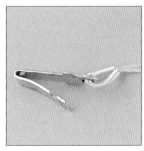

3 Now add all the remaining pearls, taking care to keep them in the right order if they are graduated by size. Finally, add the other piece of gimp and the other half of the clasp.

4 Remove the needle by cutting its loop, not the thread. You can then dispose of the needle. Hold open the loop end of the thread with your thumb and forefinger, reach down and pull the clasp and gimp that you have just added back through the loop. Tighten this up to form a ring-hitch knot, with the gimp looped to hold the clasp.

5 Slide one pearl up towards this end, flush with the loop of gimp. Then form an overhand knot as close to this pearl as possible. There is a knack to this which will come with practice. Some people find it useful to put a darning needle or tweezers into the knot to help slide it up to the pearl. Alternatively, you can try pulling the two threads in opposite directions.

Slide the next pearl up to the knot you have just made, and repeat the process above by making another overhand knot next to this pearl. Once the knots are in place either side of a pearl there should be no side-to-side movement. Make sure you make your overhand knot in the same direction each time, to keep the knots the same size and shape.

6 Continue sliding the pearls and knotting until you have two pearls left at the other end. Slide the second to last one down, but do not make a knot. The loose ends of your slip knot will be used to create this final knot. Untie the slip knot, and pull the slack out of the necklace by pulling these two ends in opposite directions, so that the remaining pearls are side by side and the gimp has formed a tight loop around the clasp.

7 Make a half-hitch knot around the central strands, then cross them round to the other side of the central strands and finish with an overhand knot. Trim this 1–2 mm from the knot, and seal with a lighter or match if you are using polyester thread, or a drop of clear nail varnish if you are using silk.

Tip: If you are using a flame to seal a knot, be careful not to singe the thread as this will make it go black. Also, make sure you only melt the tails, not the actual knot, which could make it unravel.

The finished necklace

Beading without knots

If you decide not to knot your pearls or beads, you can follow the instructions above, with some small changes.

You will need the same tools and materials; however, your thread only needs to be twice as long as your necklace, plus 40 cm extra for finishing. Otherwise, follow the instructions in steps 1 to 4 above.

When you get to step 5, slide all the beads up to the loop end. Untie the slip knot, and pull the slack out of the necklace by pulling these two ends in opposite directions, so that all the beads are side by side and the gimp has formed a tight loop around the clasp at both ends.

Using the two loose ends, finish the necklace by following the knotting instructions in step 7.

The six-row beaded cuff shown (right) was made using the technique described above, and a three-row tube clasp, by adding two rows of beads to each loop of the clasp.

A six-row cuff of smoky quartz, pearls and crystals, by Yarwood-White

You can combine your threading skills with the wire-loop technique to create interesting designs, like the mixed gemstone and crystal necklace shown below.

Gemstone and crystal necklace made with threading and wire techniques

Tip: Most necklace designs can be adapted to make matching bracelets. Do consider though that some clasps are tricky to do up with one hand, so although they look great on a necklace, they may be less suitable for a bracelet. Also bear in mind that bracelets with charms could catch on a lace or embroidered dress.

A two-row pearl choker

Chokers

Chokers are worn high and tight around the neck, and often have multiple numbers of rows. They are very glamorous, but look best on long slim necks, with swept-up hairstyles.

The simplest way to create a choker is using memory wire, as one size fits all and there is no need for a clasp. You simply thread the beads onto the wire, and use spacer bars to join two or more rows together.

For a softer look to your choker, you can string it on thread. Unless the choker is carefully made to measure, an extender clasp is essential. If the choker is too tight it will be uncomfortable; if it is too loose it will slip down the neck.

Beaded cake by Savoir Designs

6.

Other Wedding Accessories

You can apply your jewellery-making skills in many ways to create other wedding accessories with individuality and style.

Think about the theme of the wedding, and where you could add a flourish with a handmade finishing touch. Try not to simply recreate the bridal jewellery (unless the bride wants to see a mini version of her tiara on top of her cake) but use the style of her accessories and the materials as inspiration to develop your designs. For example, if you have made twinkly crystal jewellery for a winter bride, carry this theme through by creating icicle and snowflake-style table decorations.

This chapter shows you a range of ideas for creating wedding accessories, and will inspire you to develop your designs in different and imaginative ways.

STATIONERY

Hand-embellished wedding stationery is becoming increasingly popular as an alternative to traditional engraved cards. Your design can be applied to invitations, order-of-service sheets, menus, place cards, table plans, thank-you cards and any other stationery that may be needed for the wedding.

The scroll-style invitation shown right is bound using a hand-beaded wire of lilac and silver beads, and posted in a co-ordinating gift box.

A beaded scroll band, by The Whole Caboodle Design Ltd

The scroll shown left has been finished using the same sprig-style wire and bead technique covered in Chapter 4 for making tiaras and hair pins.

An invitation with a beaded sprig, by The Whole Caboodle Design Ltd

The matching invitation, favour box and place card shown left are embellished with wire scrolls and crystals.

Co-ordinating beaded stationery, by The Whole Caboodle Design Ltd

FLOWERS

There are many ways that beads and wire can be used to add interest to bouquets, buttonholes and table arrangements. Try adding clusters of beads on wire to an arrangement, or beaded leaves to buttonholes. You can also add interest to the stem of a bouquet by circling it with crystals or pearls.

In the summery bridal bouquet shown opposite, one dainty pearl has been wired into the centre of some of the blooms for an understated look.

Bouquet with wired pearls

For a more glamorous effect, diamanté stones can be nestled in a bouquet of roses and added to a simple lily buttonhole (see next page).

A bouquet of roses with diamanté, by In Water London®

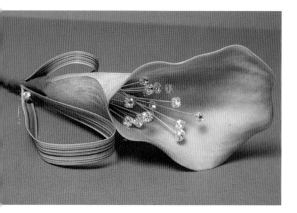

A lily buttonhole with diamanté by In Water London®

For young bridesmaids, a wire and beaded fairy wand is a fun alternative to flowers.

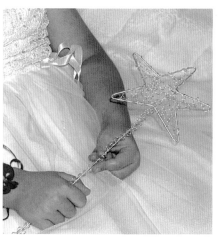

Beaded fairy wand, by Loves Me Loves Me Knot

AT THE RECEPTION

The wedding cake is often a centrepiece at the reception, so it is a great place to go to town with the decorations. A simple tiered cake can be transformed into something quite spectacular, by adding a handmade garland of beads, or an unusual cake topper.

Sprays of pink and clear beads encircle the tiers of this cake, by Juliana Dutton

Sprays of beads explode like fireworks from this fun cake, by Tracey Mann

Beaded napkin rings are a beautiful finishing touch to a table setting, and can be colour-co-ordinated to tone with the setting or add a splash of vibrant colour. They are best strung on strong beading elastic.

Napkins can also be fastened by twisting wire into a decorative shape. Here wired raffia has been used to create naive heart shapes for a rustic wedding.

Silver pearl and crystal napkin ring, by Yarwood-White

Tip: Napkin rings can double as favours for wedding guests, who can take them home as a personal memento of the day.

Napkins tied with wired raffia, by Loves Me Loves Me Knot

Beaded garlands also look pretty strung around candle holders, where they reflect the light for extra twinkle.

Wine-glass charms not only look pretty, but help guests to identify their own glass.

Beaded tealight holder, by Loves Me Loves Me Knot

Wine-glass charms. Photo by permission of Wedding Ideas Magazine, Giraffe Media Ltd

7.

Building a Bridal Jewellery Business

If you have been inspired by the skills you have learned so far, you may well be wondering if you could use them to run your own business making and selling bridal jewellery.

With some careful planning and a great deal of hard work your jewellery business could be a big success.

This chapter covers what you will need to consider before taking the plunge. There are many good resources that explore these points in much more detail, and further reading is strongly recommended (see pp. 94-5).

BUSINESS PLANNING

A great way to start thinking about your business is to sit down and write a business plan. This will help you to consolidate your thoughts and consider your goals, and how you plan to reach them.

You can change your business plan when you need to, so do not worry too much if you don't have all the answers. In fact, it will be important for you to review your plan at least every three months during the early stages of your business, as you adapt to experiences and opportunities. Think of your business plan as a constantly evolving tool that will help you keep your business on track.

Your business plan should include the following:

- A description of the business: What is the purpose of the business, what will it exist to do? How will you run the business, i.e. will you be a sole trader (self-employed), a partnership or a limited company? Will you start the business whilst still working in a part-time or full-time job to help with funding?
- A description of the product: What type of jewellery will you produce, and why will it be different or distinctive? How will it be manufactured and with what type of materials? What will the price range be?
- A description of your target market: What type of bride are you aiming at? What will be her age, style and price range? Will you also make jewellery for grooms and attendants?

- A competitive analysis: Who are your competitors, and what are their strengths and weaknesses? How well established are they, where do they sell and how do they promote themselves?
- A marketing strategy and plan: How will you tell your target market about your jewellery? Will you use advertising, PR, direct mail, a website, exhibitions or a combination of these? What are the costs involved? Are there seasonal factors to consider?
- A sales strategy: Will you sell direct to customers, through retailers, online or through exhibitions? What level of sales do you hope to achieve?
- An operations strategy: Will you need to employ people, where will you work from, what facilities/equipment will you need?
- A finance plan: How much money will you need to start the business? What are your cash-flow projections? How do you plan to raise any additional funding you need?
- A description of the future of the business: where would you like the business to be in six months, one year, two years and five years?

The following information should help you answer some of the questions above.

TYPE OF BUSINESS

There are a number of ways to start your business. Few people are in the fortunate financial position of being able to leave their current job or lifestyle to finance a business with a large injection of cash.

However, because some bridal jewellery can be made from home with a few small tools, it is relatively straightforward to build a business slowly and carefully around your current employment, without having to take huge financial risks.

There are several different structures your business can take, and each one has its advantages and disadvantages. It is worth considering the best structure for you, as it will affect the tax you pay, your financial liability and the way you make decisions about your business. For each of the business types described below, you will need to consult the relevant small-business laws and tax regulations in your own country. This information is for the U.K. only.

Sole trader

This is the simplest way to run a business if you are working alone. There are no set-up costs and your profits will be taxed as income. You need to register as self-employed with HM Revenue and Customs, and complete a tax return every year.

You will need to pay fixed-rate Class 2 National Insurance Contributions (NICs), and Class 4 NICs on your profits. You will be personally liable for any debts your business runs up.

Partnership

Two or more people can form a partnership to share the running costs and profits of a business. The partners will be self-employed as above, and tax and National Insurance are paid in the same way by each partner. Each partner is personally liable for the whole of any debts run up by the business. It is important to seek legal advice when forming a partnership and draw up a written agreement to avoid disputes, even if you form a partnership with a close friend or family member.

Limited-liability company

Limited companies exist as an entity distinct from their shareholders. This means your personal finances are separated from those of the business, and you are not personally liable for company debts. You must have at least one director, and a company secretary.

You will need to pay to register the company at Companies House, and submit an annual return once a year. Your company will submit a tax return and will pay corporation tax on its profits. Directors and employees will pay tax on their salaries.

PRICING

Pricing is a notoriously tricky area, but it is vital to get it right or your business will not survive. For every piece of jewellery you design and make you will need to work out a wholesale price and a retail price.

Wholesale price/cost price

The wholesale price or cost price is based on the amount that it costs you to make the product, with a margin for profit included. This is the absolute minimum that you can afford to sell a piece of work for. Any less than this and you will be simply throwing money away.

The wholesale price is calculated using the following formula:

Materials + Labour + Overhead + % Profit Margin = Wholesale Price

Tip: Only offer your wholesale price to bona-fide resellers, and stipulate a minimum order either in money or in number of items to ensure your buyers are genuine.

Retail price

The retail price is the price that the customer will ultimately pay. If you sell your work to a shop at the wholesale price, they will mark this up by anything between 100% and 250%.

The retail price is calculated using the following formula:
Wholesale Price + 150% = Retail Price

This mark-up may seem extreme, but you do need to take into account the overheads of the shop and the expenses they incur in selling your work.

If you sell your work direct to the customer, you should also add this mark-up. You will have to decide whether you prefer to sell in larger quantities at a wholesale price, or direct to the customer with a much higher profit margin, but incurring the time and expense of reaching and selling to those customers.

If you decide to do both – sell to retailers and also direct to customers through exhibitions – it is important that you keep the retail price as consistent as possible. By undercutting your retailers with similar products you risk upsetting them and their customers, and damaging your reputation.

If your business is VAT-registered, you must also add 17.5% to your retail price (this is covered in more detail later in this chapter).

Costing your labour

The old adage 'time is money' applies here. The more time you put into a piece of jewellery, the more you need to charge for it.

When working out how much you need to earn per hour, it is important to remember that there are only so many hours in the day that you can be making jewellery, and if you are not making jewellery, you are not making money. However, you still need to allow time to market and sell that jewellery, and to run your business. If you do nothing but make jewellery all day, you won't sell any.

On that basis it is likely that out of an eight-hour working day, you will probably only be making jewellery for five of those hours, or 25 hours per week. Allowing for holidays and illness, you can probably be making jewellery for 48 out of 52 weeks in a year.

If your hourly rate was £15, that would give you the annual income below:

25 hours/week x 48 weeks = 1200 hours per year x £15 = £18,000 p.a.

You then need to ask yourself if £18,000 per year is enough to cover your personal expenses such as mortgage/rent, food, bills and other expenses.

Alternatively, you could total your annual expenses, and use this to calculate the hourly rate you need to earn.

Costing your business overheads

Overheads are all the costs involved in running your business. It can be tricky to estimate what these costs will be when you are setting up a business, but with some research you can get a good idea. It is better to overestimate rather than underestimate your costs, so round up if you are unsure and add a percentage for contingency.

Some costs to consider are:

- Rent
- Telephone
- Broadband
- IT services/software
- Tools/equipment
- Lighting/heating/water
- Business rates
- Insurance
- Postage
- Stationery
- Legal/accountancy fees
- Bank charges
- Website hosting
- Domain registration
- Marketing
- Advertising
- Photography
- Travel
- Exhibition costs

Estimate these costs on an annual basis, then divide by the same number of hours you used to calculate your labour. For example:

Total overheads: £10,000 / 1200 hours per year = £8.33 per hour
(round up to £9)

As an example, let's say you need to calculate the price of a tiara:

- Cost of materials (beads, wire, ribbon, packaging)   £6.00
- Labour (2 hours at £15 per hour)   £30.00
- Overheads (2 hours at £9 per hour)   £18.00
- Subtotal   £54.00
- Plus Profit 20%   £10.80
- Wholesale Price   £64.80
- Plus 100% mark-up   £64.80
- Retail Price   £129.60
(round up to £130)

COMPETITOR ANALYSIS

It is best not to get too obsessed with what your competitors are doing, as this can mean you spend more time worrying about them than you do concentrating on your own business. However, you do need to know what other options your customers have to choose from, and use this to make sure you are always offering your customers the best you can.

Make a list of your competitors. Look at their websites, advertising, brochures, packaging, pricing and product ranges and comment on what you think they do well and not so well. Work out how you can offer something better and, importantly, different from your competitors.

MARKET RESEARCH

You can research your market in a number of ways:

- Visit bridal retailers and jewellery boutiques.
- Search the Internet to see who else is selling your type of jewellery.
- Read bridal magazines and trade magazines.
- Visit trade fairs and bridal exhibitions.
- Talk to friends about the jewellery they wore on their wedding day.

Start collecting this information together to help you paint a picture of the market, and where your jewellery will fit in. By identifying a gap in the market, you will find it easier to differentiate your products and attract attention to them.

You will also be able to work out where and how best to sell your products. Do you want to focus on bespoke commissions and sell face-to-face to a local market? Or would you rather operate a mail order or Internet sales business, and sell your jewellery nationally or even internationally?

Target customers

Researching your market will help you establish who your target customer is, and therefore refine your products and services to suit her.

Obviously your primary target is going to be brides, but of course not all brides are the same. If your designs are traditional tiaras, or outrageous feather creations, they will be worn by a different type of bride.

Stay focussed on your target customer, rather than trying to be all things to all people, which can leave you with an unclear business proposition and customers who are confused about exactly what you are good at.

If you decide to sell your jewellery to retailers, you need to research which outlets have a target customer similar to your own. Your jewellery will need to work with the style of the retailer's dresses, and be an appropriate price for their customers.

Tip: Create a profile of your ideal customer. Give her a name, an age, and write a list of her likes and dislikes, where she lives and shops, and what magazines she reads. Think of her when designing and marketing your jewellery to help you focus on your business proposition.

MARKETING

Marketing is all about communication; making sure that your target market is aware of your jewellery and why they should buy it. A number of elements go to make up your 'marketing mix', and you will create the mix depending on your own objectives and budget.

Branding

Once you have established who your target market is, you can start to think about your branding. Your brand is the personality of your business, and should be consistent across all your communications with customers.

Decide on the personality you want your business to project, based on your market research and target customer. For example, do you want a fun and light-hearted brand to appeal to a younger bride with a relaxed outlook on life? Or do you want to go for a classic, traditional brand that you can sell to upmarket boutiques?

Write a short brand statement, explaining the personality of your brand and the key messages you want your branding to communicate. Pin this on the wall and use it as a benchmark for all your communications.

The following elements of your brand all 'say' something about your business. Spend some time working out the best way to produce them in line with your brand statement:

- Name of your business
- Logo
- Tone of voice (writing style)
- Typeface
- Colours
- Stationery (letterhead, compliment slips, business cards, envelopes)
- Website design

- Photography
- Packaging
- Promotional material (brochures, postcards, advertisements)
- Signage
- Product display.

Public relations

When you communicate with your 'public' through media such as newspapers, magazines, radio, events or even TV, without paying for the space, this is public relations (PR).

PR is a great way to build your reputation among customers, retailers and the market as a whole. Unlike advertising it has the benefit of coming from a third party (usually a journalist or publication) and so can carry more authority with the reader.

Having said that, you have less control over what is said about your business than with advertising, and you need to come up with newsworthy and interesting information to get the coverage you want.

There are many PR agencies that can help with this, but they are not cheap, and you may find you need to do some of your own PR when you first start your business.

Start by compiling a list of target media. This should include wedding magazines and websites, and trade magazines if you are targeting retailers. You may also want to target non-wedding magazines that may include wedding features. Call them to establish the name and contact details of the most relevant journalist or editor. Ask how they prefer to receive information (by email or post) and what their copy deadline is each week/month.

If you have news such as the launch of a new collection, a forthcoming exhibition or an award win, write a press release. This should be a short, snappy one-page document, and must include the following information:

- A headline
- A release date, or 'for immediate release' if the information is not time-sensitive
- The five Ws: Who, What, Where, When and Why
- A relevant quote, from you or a third party
- Contact details for further information
- High-resolution images.

Tip: Be prepared to send sample products to magazines for photoshoots, which they often request at short notice.

Then it is a question of building relationships with journalists until eventually they think of you first when they need your type of jewellery.

Advertising

It is easy to waste a lot of money on advertising, if it is done carelessly. However, it is an important part of your marketing mix and if done properly will create awareness and sales for you.

Before you commit to any advertising space, think carefully about your objectives. Are you trying to attract new buyers, launch a new product or highlight a special promotion?

Put together a schedule for the year, with a budget for advertising. You can then work out when you will need to be advertising, and how much you can afford to spend. For example, you may want to advertise your 'Snow Queen' range of crystal jewellery in October, to catch the brides shopping for winter weddings.

Contact the advertising media that you think will reach your target market and ask for a media pack. This will include details of their circulation and readership, audience profile and ratecard costs. You can often negotiate a significant discount off the ratecard cost, especially if you commit to a series of adverts. The most appropriate media will probably be the same wedding magazines or websites that you targeted for PR.

Before you book your space, do a quick calculation to work out how many pieces of jewellery you would need to produce and sell to cover the cost of the advert. This can help make the decision for you, if you think it is a realistic number.

Once you have chosen your media, you will need to think carefully about the content of your advertisement. Include a well-lit, high-resolution photograph, contact details, and a clear message with a call to action. Less is more, and your advert will have more impact if you don't try to cram too many words or pictures into it.

Tip: Don't forget to budget for production costs, such as photography, design and artwork, or ask the magazine for help producing your copy when you book your space. They will often provide this service free of charge.

Bear in mind that money spent on advertising will come out of your overall marketing budget, and therefore could be spent on other marketing activities such as direct mail, exhibitions or employing a PR consultant.

Database marketing

It is essential that you keep a database of all the enquiries you receive, as this is valuable information. Brides can sometimes take months to make a decision on their accessories, and during this time you can keep in touch and work to convert those enquiries into sales. You can also analyse the information to see what products are selling, and where your customers are coming from.

Your database can be a simple spreadsheet, or if you have the facility you can use a database software package. Here is an example of the type of information you should collect:

Name	Sandra Brown
Address	30 St James Park, Anytown, AB1 2CD
Telephone	0123 456 7890
Email	sandra@email.com
Date of wedding	01/09/2009
Source	Friend
Item(s) bought	Snow Queen tiara
Total price	130
Notes	May want earrings to match, follow up in July

Ask your customers how they heard about you – from a friend, advert, at an exhibition – and include this information under 'source'.

You can follow up enquiries on your database in a number of ways. The key is to make regular contact so that when they are ready to buy, they think of you. You could send the following:

- Details of new designs
- Promotions or special offers
- Details of forthcoming exhibitions
- Press coverage
- Testimonials from other happy customers.

Once a bride has bought from you, there are a number of reasons to make contact. You could send the following:

- Details of matching items
- Suggestions for bridesmaids' gifts, which are often left to the last minute
- A feedback form, to find out how you could improve your products or service
- Congratulations after her wedding
- A request for a photo of her on the wedding day for your portfolio.

The bridal business is different to other businesses as it is obviously unlikely that you will obtain a repeat order from a bride. However, it is an industry built on word-of-mouth referrals, so by building relationships and keeping in touch with your brides after their wedding, you will make it easier for them to tell their friends about you.

> **Tip:** In the UK, if you are storing information about your customers on a database, you have a legal requirement to comply with the Data Protection Act 1998. You can find out more from the Information Commissioner's Office at www.ico.gov.uk, or call the helpline on 01625 545745. If you are based elsewhere you should check, and comply with, that country's relevant legislation.

Websites

If you are planning to sell directly to customers, a website will be a valuable tool. It could simply be a few pages with photographs of your work and contact details, which acts as an online brochure. A website like this can be set up relatively easily and inexpensively.

At the other end of the spectrum you could run an e-commerce website, which allows customers to shop online for your jewellery using a credit card, and will automate some or all of the sales process for you.

If you are new to websites, talk to friends who may have been through the process, or if you see a website you admire, contact the company to find out who built it.

It is worth asking for a content management system (CMS) when you speak to website designers. A CMS is software that will allow you to easily update your website yourself as often as you wish. This avoids having to go back to the web designer every time, which can be slow and costly, and means your website can easily become out of date.

Exhibitions

Wedding shows and trade fairs can be used as an opportunity to promote your business, and sell your jewellery. They vary in cost and in professionalism, so if possible try visiting a show before you book a stand.

To make the most of your opportunity and to budget accurately, consider the following when planning to exhibit:

- The amount of stock you will need
- Promotional material, e.g. business cards, brochures, postcards and price lists
- Stand extras such as lighting, electricity and furniture
- How to display your work, and signage for your stand

- How you will record customer details
- Transport, accommodation and meals
- Help on the stand (you will need to leave it for comfort breaks)
- Insurance for your work/security arrangements
- Press packs for the press office
- Advertising in the show guide, or sponsorship/fashion-show opportunities.

Photography

In most marketing activities, the quality of your photography is crucial. If possible, it is worth paying a professional photographer to obtain a few high-quality shots, as these will make a big difference to the quality of your marketing materials.

If this is not possible, there are a number of things you can do to improve the results of your own photography:

- Use a digital camera to allow plenty of trial and error
- Use a tripod
- Keep backgrounds plain, and try different colours
- Photograph against a roll of card to achieve a seamless background
- Make sure you have plenty of light, and avoid flash photography
- Use double-sided tape to secure pieces.

Also, ask your brides for a wedding photo that shows off the jewellery, which will probably have been taken by a professional photographer.

SELLING YOUR WORK

Selling direct to customers

We covered the consulting process in detail in Chapter 1. If you choose to work this way, you will need to attract customers using your marketing mix, and sell through a website, bridal exhibitions or your own shop or studio.

Selling wholesale

This means selling your product to a bridal shop, department store, gallery or other retailer who will in turn sell it to the end customer.

Do your research before approaching an outlet to make sure your product is suitable for their target market. Call and ask to make an appointment to show your samples to the jewellery buyer.
When you meet the buyer, have your samples well presented and organised, and be prepared to answer questions about your wholesale

price, recommended retail price and delivery times, as well as about your product and how it is made.

Some retailers may want to work on a sale-or-return (SOR) basis. This means that they display your work, and they pay you the agreed percentage when it sells. The work remains your property until it sells, so it is very important to provide a clear delivery note with prices and terms of trading when you deliver your work.

SOR is a good way to get your work into retailers and prove that it sells, as there is no risk to the retailer. However, you do need to be organised to keep track of your stock, and keep in regular contact with the retailer to make sure your work is on display, in good condition, and that you are paid promptly for work that has sold.

Display

Whether you are showing your work at an exhibition, trade show or in a shop, it pays to think carefully about your display.

It is important that customers can see your jewellery clearly, so do not overcrowd your display, and keep any props discreet so that they don't attract more attention than your designs. Use plenty of lighting to highlight your jewellery and make the crystals sparkle.

Visit jewellery departments and boutiques and notice where you see good or bad displays. The props, colours, lighting, height and angle of the jewellery, photography and overall arrangement all contribute to the success of the display.

BUSINESS ADMINISTRATION

Raising finance

When you start your business you will need money to buy tools and materials, and to cover your overheads until you start earning income. If you don't have access to savings, you will have to raise this money in another way, usually through investors, loans or grants.

Investors will give you money in return for a share of your business profits. You can raise investment through venture capitalists, business angels or through friends and family.

Loans can be arranged through your bank, building society or an authorised lender, but do shop around and compare interest rates and terms before committing to an agreement.

Grants do not need to be repaid, and do not involve giving away a share of your profits, but you will need to meet certain eligibility criteria to apply. Grants are offered by government bodies, local authorities and some charities, so you need to research what is available to you based on your circumstances and location.

Cash flow

A cash-flow forecast will help you work out how much money you will have coming in and going out of your business on a monthly basis. It can help you identify peaks and troughs in your business, and alert you to any periods where you may need to borrow extra funds to cover your expenses. Although at first it will be based on your best estimates, it is always a worthwhile exercise and can be crucial to the survival of your business.

Bookkeeping

You can record your accounting information by hand in a ledger, or on a spreadsheet or accounting software package. Whichever system you use, you will make life easier for yourself by getting into good habits from the start and being methodical and organised.

You need to record all your sales, including whether or not you have been paid the money you are owed. You also need to record all your purchases, and keep the corresponding receipts filed in order.

It is helpful to assign each purchase with a category (e.g. overheads, materials, postage, marketing) and each sale with information about its source (e.g. advertising, word of mouth). This will help you work out where your money is coming from and going to.

Whether you are a sole trader, in a partnership or have a limited company, you will need this information to complete your tax return.

VAT (UK only)

You do not need to register for VAT (although you can do so voluntarily) unless your sales in the previous 12 months are over a certain level (£61,000 in 2006) or are expected to reach that level in the next 30 days.

If you are VAT-registered, you need to charge VAT on all your sales (which you then pay to HM Revenue and Customs), but you will also be able to reclaim the VAT you have paid on your outgoings.

If you are registered, you must issue VAT receipts/invoices on all your sales, and keep VAT receipts for all your expenses. You will record the VAT charged/paid on each entry when bookkeeping, and submit VAT returns to HM Revenue and Customs.

If you are based outside the UK, you will need to find out about your country's relevant tax rules.

Insurance

There are a number of types of insurance you may need for your business:

> **Tip:** Your household insurance may be invalid if you work from home, so get in touch with your insurance company to discuss extending your policy.

- Buildings insurance to cover your business premises against fire, flood and other damage.
- Contents insurance for your stock, tools and other business equipment (check whether this will cover your stock when away from your usual place of business).
- Goods-in-transit insurance to cover your stock when travelling to and from exhibitions.
- If you use your car for business purposes, you must inform your motor insurance company.
- If you employ staff, employers' liability insurance is compulsory by law.
- Public-liability insurance covers damages awarded to a member of the public for injury or damage which occurs as a result of your business activities.
- Product-liability insurance covers damages awarded to a member of the public for injury or damage which occurs as a result of defects in the design or manufacture of your products.
- You may also want to consider personal-accident and sickness insurance, income protection, medical insurance and life insurance to protect you or your family if you are unable to work.

Intellectual property

Your designs can be protected by copyright in the form of drawings or photographs; simply add the copyright symbol © followed by your name or company name if you are a limited company, and the current year.

You can also register a design with the Patent Office, for a fee of £60. The design must be new and different from anything that has previously been on the market to qualify.

It may be worth having your trading name or company name and logo trademarked. This protects you from other companies in your business category using similar names or logo designs.

Hallmarking

Precious metal items such as wedding or engagement rings will need to be hallmarked before you sell them. You will need to register your own personal mark with an Assay Office (in London, Birmingham, Edinburgh or Sheffield). You will then send your items to the office, where they will test the quality of the metal, and mark the item to indicate that it exceeds the minimum standard of purity.

Health and safety

Employers, employees and the self-employed all have a legal obligation to prevent people from being harmed by work or becoming ill through work. Health and safety laws apply to all businesses, however small. There is a basic guide available for small businesses through the Health and Safety Executive which explains what steps you should take to make sure you comply with the law.

Further Reading

Jeweller's Directory of Gemstones, Judith Crowe, A&C Black
Diamonds, Marijan Dundek, Noble Gems Publications
Diamond Ring Buying Guide, Renee Newman, International Jewelry
    Publications
Pearl Buying Guide, Renee Newman, International Jewelry Publications
The Pearl Book: The Definitive Buying Guide, Antoinette Matlins,
    Gemstone Press
Basic Jewellery Making Techniques, Jinks McGrath, A&C Black
Handbook of Jewellery Techniques, Carles Codina, A&C Black
Jewellery Making Techniques Book, Elizabeth Oliver, Apple
Rings, Jinks McGrath, A&C Black
Wire Jewellery, Hans Stofer, A&C Black
Bead and Wire Art Jewellery, J. Marsha Michler, KP Books
Tiaras: Past and Present, Geoffrey Munn, V&A Publications
Tiaras, Diana Scarisbrick, Chronicle Books
Timeless Tiaras: Chaumet from 1904 to the Present, Diana Scarisbrick,
    Editions Assouline
Running a Workshop, Barclay Price, Crafts Council
Craft & Art – the Business, Elizabeth White, Elliot Right Way Books
Marketing and Selling Your Handmade Jewelry, Vicki Lareau,
    Interweave Press Inc

Business Resources

General business advice: Business Link, www.businesslink.gov.uk

Data Protection Act: Information Commissioners Office, www.ico.gov.uk
Tax issues: HM Revenue & Customs, www.hmrc.gov.uk
Insurance: Association of British Insurers, www.abi.org.uk
Registering designs, trademarks and copyright: The UK Patent Office,
    www.patent.gov.uk
Legal matters: Lawyers for your Business (Law Society),
    www.lfyb.lawsociety.org.uk
Hallmarking: British Hallmarking Council,
    www.britishhallmarkingcouncil.gov.uk
Health and Safety: Heath and Safety Executive, www.hse.gov.uk

Training

For a list of nationwide colleges and independent companies offering courses in jewellery design and making, contact:

The Jewellery and Allied Industries Training Council (JAITC)
c/o British Jewellers' Association
10 Vyse Street
BirminghamB18 6LT
Website: www.jaitc.org.uk

Picture credits

p.6 – © istockphoto.com/Daniel Vineyard; p.8 – © Christine Cowdell; p.9 – © Clare Yarwood-White; p.10 – © Christine Cowdell; p.13 – © istockphoto.com/Veronica Munsey; p.14 – © istockphoto.com/Luba Nel; p.15 – (top left) © istockphoto.com/Eric Renard, (main picture) © istockphoto.com/David Freund; p.17 – © istockphoto.com/Franziska Lang; p.18 – © Christine Cowdell; p.20 – (top left) © Susan Astaire, (right) © istockphoto.com/ Guillermo Lobo; p.21 – © Christine Cowdell; p.22 – (top) © Clare Yarwood-White (bottom) © Clare Yarwood-White; p.23 – © Clare Yarwood-White; p.25 – (all) © Clare Yarwood-White; p.26 – ©istockphoto.com/ Joey Nelson; p.27 – © istockphoto.com/Daniel Vineyard; p.28 – © istockphoto.com/elen8; p.29 © istockphoto.com/Daniel Vineyard; p.31 – © Bill Prentice; p.32 – © istockphoto.com/angelhell; p.33 – © istockphoto.com/mirajewel; p.34 – © Bill Prentice; p.35 – © istockphoto/Tracey Cullen; p.36 – © Bill Prentice; p.37 – © Susan Astaire; p.38 – (top) © istockphoto.com/roadpicture (bottom) © Susan Astaire; p.39 (both) – © Susan Astaire; p.40 – © Christine Cowdell; p.41 – (tiara) © Clare Yarwood-White, (headband) © Christine Cowdell; p42 – (hair pin and crown) © Clare Yarwood-White, (others) © Christine Cowdell; pp.45-53 – © Clare Yarwood-White; p.54 – © Christine Cowdell; p. 55 – © Clare Yarwood-White; p.56 – (top and middle) © Clare Yarwood-White, (bottom) © Christine Cowdell; p.57 – © istockphoto.com/Wilson Valentin; p.58 – (all) © Clare Yarwood-White; p.59 – (top) © Clare Yarwood-White, (bottom) © istockphoto.com/Wilson Valentin; p.60-65 – © Clare Yarwood-White; p.66 – © istockphoto.com/bmcent1; p.67 – © istockphoto.com/Sandra O'Claire; p.68 – © Savoir Design; p.69 – © Mark Gawthorne; p.70 – (top) © Mark Gawthorne, (bottom) © The Whole Caboodle Design Ltd; p.71 – (top) © istockphoto.com/dtsuneo, (bottom) © In Water; p.72 – (top left) © In Water, (top right) © Loves Me Loves Me Knot, (bottom left) © Alister Thorpe; p.73 – © Alister Thorpe; p.74 – (top) © Christine Cowdell, (bottom) © Botanique Editions; p.75 – (top) © Boltze,(bottom) © Donna Berridge. (Wine glass charms: Breast cancer awareness charm and Wedded Bliss charm,www.wendyswinecharms.co.uk; bow-shaped charm, www.halo-s.co.uk; crystal heart on gold wire, www.helpthebride.com; star bead with pearls, www.turquoiseweddings.co.uk; pearls with shell heart, www.cammardesigns.co.uk.) P.76 – © Christine Cowdell; p.93 – © istockphoto.com/Dominik Damaziak.

Index